HOW ROAD RACERS TRAIN

by
Greg Brock

First Printing, January 1980

Production Staff: Grace Light, Alicia Phillips, Suzie Carlyon.

Jacket Design: Ann Harris.

Library of Congress Catalog Card Number: 77-94968
Standard Book Number: 0-911520-84-8.

Printed in the United States of America.

PHOTO CREDITS

4	Gwyn Adams
9	Jeff Johnson
18	Steven E. Sutton/Duomo
21	Cindy Brown
30	Jeff Reinking
34	Kraig Scattarella
40	Bill Leung, Jr.
42	Steven E. Sutton/Duomo
43	Joe Arrazola
44	Jeff Johnson
47	Doug Wells
48	Kevin Knight
53	Natural Light beer
56	Steven E. Sutton/Duomo
59	Jim Engle
62	David M. Benyak
67	Jeff Johnson
73	L'eggs Mini Marathon
75	Mike Spinelli
84	Jeff Johnson

TABLE OF CONTENTS

ABOUT THE AUTHOR

Greg Brock brings a rich background as athlete, coach, and author to the writing of *How Road Racers Train*.

As an athlete at Stanford University, Brock held school records in the 2-, 3-, and 6-mile, and was an All-American in cross country in '68 and '69. No stranger to road racing, Greg finished fifth in the 1972 Olympic Trials Marathon.

Now head track and cross country coach at Santa Cruz High School in California, Brock has five league championships in three years to his credit, all on a program geared to the long-time participation of his athletes.

Greg is perhaps best known for his popular book, *How High School Runners Train* (Tafnews Press, 1976). He has now turned his critical eye to the world of the road racer, and while most of the programs are from the elite of distance running, the author has taken care to include several classes of athletes in *HRRT*, in keeping with his philosophy of this book as a "forum of ideas about training" for runners of all levels.

INTRODUCTION

What! Another "How they train book"? Just what is the value of a simplistic look into the training methods of a few selected runners? It could be a shallow attempt on the part of the author to cash in on a little of the money to be made from the running boom. This argument shouldn't be totally discounted but it really isn't very much money.

The main justification for this book is that it can create a forum of ideas about training and the road running lifestyle for the novice racer as well as the elite runner. By examining the training programs of others, an individual can critically evaluate his own program. It is a catalyst for new ideas. The runner can see how others deal with situations similar to his own.

This book is about road racing, an activity which is now enjoying an unprecedented boom in this country after many years of being the least popular of the three running sports. Track racing was long the most popular because of its wide range of events, from sprints to distances. Cross country was developed in America around the school system, as much to give coaches fall employment as to increase the base off-season mileage of the runners. Strict road racing, not the cross-continent type or six-day variety, gained strength with the introduction of the modern Olympics and the marathon.

An interesting aspect of road racing is that it is much more like track running than cross country. It is run on a hard, relatively even surface. Cross country is on a softer, uneven surface and requires far greater agility.

Road running is a mass phenomenon in this country right now. In this book we're looking for a cross section, not just the top runners. We want to address the universality of road racing and find how we are similar, not different. A major concern is to develop a feeling for how successful runners/racers integrate running into their lifestyles.

Who is a road racer? Anyone who steps into a race is a racer. This question is like the one about the difference between "running" and "jogging." If a person achieves a position of having both feet simultaneously off the ground, unlike walking where one foot is always in contact with the ground, that person is a runner, and we don't need to talk about joggers. To put it simply, a person decides what to label himself.

What about the fitness runner? There is a major difference between running for fitness and running for the ultimate performance. Training roughly 5 miles per day, with the heart rate elevated to 75-80% of its maximum capacity, a person can achieve 90% of his racing capability. At this stage a person is very fit. But, if an athlete wants to achieve the last 5-10% in terms of competitive performance, the quality and quantity are greatly increased and so is the chance of injury. A person can be a racer and a fitness runner. Each individual must decide on the level of excellence in racing he wishes to attain.

One of the reasons for the popularity of road racing in this country is the changing values of the culture. It used to be that success was narrowly defined as winning. Not everyone can be an Olympic champion. The value of the running movement in this country is that there is now the feeling that to finish a race is the measure of success, or to run a "perfect race" according to individual goals. Achievement in our society has long been measured by material success. The change toward a kind of spiritual self-satisfaction has been heralded, paradoxically, by the commercials of many leading materialist institutions. "Go for the Gusto!" "You Only Go Around Once" are the cries of a kind of new hedonistic existentialism. Regardless of the source, people are getting in touch with their bodies and exploring their limits. Road racers are in the vanguard of this movement.

In this book, most of the participants were and still are excellent track runners. What will be the long range effects of mass road racing on American track? Road racing has the potential to be detrimental or beneficial on America's elite distance runners. If the better runners race the roads indiscriminantly and too frequently, their track performances will suffer. However, used wisely, training for and racing the roads is an excellent way to build a foundation in a year-round systematic training regimen.

Another effect of road racing is that it is providing another entry into the running scene. Some of these people will have talent for track racing. Road racing also provides competition for the post college runner. This helps the person who matures later than college age. Interestingly, the mass running movement is providing a livelihood for many runners. Many have running stores, work for shoe or sporting goods companies or have developed their own lines of running apparel. Many of the better runners also generate income by speaking at clinics and attending or organizing running camps.

As running has become more sociably acceptable more people are trying it. This can only help the high school cross country and track coaches in their recruiting efforts. The most important point here is that there are the three types of racing; road, track and cross country. At each point of a racing season or career the emphasis on each needs evaluation. Each can make a major contribution to the total development of the runner. Cross country builds strength, hill running technique and agility; track develops speed and the ability to run at set paces; road racing is the focus for an endurance base as well as working at a hard, set pace.

Hopefully, this book will help some runners in their own training programs. It can be a source of new ideas and different ways of perceiving the training/racing situation. It can also be motivational or inspirational: we identify with others like ourselves. By sharing the ideas and experiences of others our own running experience is enhanced.

—Greg Brock

JON ANDERSON

Jon was a member of the 1972 Olympic team in the 10,000 and was the winner of the '73 Boston Marathon. Now coming back from operations on both Achilles tendons, Anderson is an example of the big, strong, slow runner, who gets the job done.

JON PETER ANDERSON: Eugene, Oregon. 6'2", 160. Born October 12, 1949 in Eugene, Oregon. Occupation: Editorial Assistant working 32.5 hrs. per week. Married with one child. Started running at age 17 and road running at 21. He plans to continue a long time. Favorite distance is 10-15 miles. Coach/advisor is Bill Bowerman.

BEST MARKS: 1500m, 3:50.2(75); Mile, 4:12. (75); 3000, 8:09.5(73); 2-mile, 8:45.4(75); 3-mile, 13:18.6(72); 5000, 13:45.8(72); 3000 SC, 9:00.9(70); 6-mile, 27:40.2(73); 10,000, 28:34.2(72); 10M, 48:25(77); Hour, 12mi 618 yds(77); 20k road, 1:01:40; 20M, 1:43:00(72); Marathon, 2:15:53.

TRAINING: Jon usually trains twice a day and once on Sunday. He runs the morning run at 7:00 a.m., missing about one day a week. His longest training run is about 30 miles. He prefers a maximum of one race every two weeks unless running shorter track races (1-3 miles). His current system involves one interval session, 1 fartlek and 1 long run per week and putting in 100-110 miles per week total.
Mon—Easy day—8 miles according to feel with some 110s and jogging between.

Tues—Intervals on soft surface. Cover 3-4 miles—variable pace—also some distance with each workout. Run—jog—after. Sometimes hill repeats are done instead of flat intervals.
Wed—Easy, like Monday.
Thurs—Fartlek—10-12 miles of varied pace running on a hilly course. This is usually done at hard pace unless racing on Saturday.
Fri—Easy, like Monday.
Sat—Race or workout according to feeling. Maybe LSD run of 10 in the morning and short fast run in afternoon.
Sun—Long run of 20-30 miles depending on upcoming competition, etc. Usually builds to 30 miles, 3-4 weeks prior to marathon. All morning runs are 3-6 miles, as he feels.

Jon's training cycles are hard day/easy day as well as hard/easy weeks. He builds up to marathons by increasing the length of his Sunday run. Anderson feels one secret is in approach to rest before a race. Too many runners do not know how to rest before a major competition.

I run because running is what I am best at and is what I enjoy most in a day-to-day routine. Having not run since August, I find the competitive fire burning more intensely all the time. Can't wait for a return. Never see an end to my running days (and therefore competitive days), as my day is not complete without a run. Have also had a great time while at it—travel, Olympics, meeting many friends (and very few enemies) emotional ups and downs; the list could go on and on.

CHRIS BERKA

An advocate of gentle training, Berka embodies the runner who believes that moderate success is obtainable without running dominating one's life.

CHRIS BERKA: Los Altos, Calif. 6'2", 160. Born May 15, 1954 in Palo Alto, Calif. Occupation: Law student. Started competing at 15 and road racing at 16. His goal is to try to always be fit for when the spirit moves him to race. Chris's favorite distance is the marathon and his advisor is Mike Ignatius.

TRAINING: Chris presently trains once a day, 365 days per year. In high school and college he ran twice a day. His longest ever run was 29 miles due to a wrong turn in a marathon. He likes to race twice a year.

BEST MARKS: Mile, 4:22(72); 2-mile, 9:26(71); 6-mile, 31:01(71); Roads: 5M, 24:25(77); 20k, 1:05(76); 25k, 1:23(74); Marathon, 2:19:48(77).

TRAINING: Ideal Week—"Training" portion of cycle

Mon—5-mile jog to loosen up.
Tues—15 miles on hilly roads at 6:30 pace.
Wed—10 miles of spontaneous fartlek on golf course.
Thurs—8 miles on flat roads at 6:30 pace.
Fri—15 miles on hilly roads at 6:00 pace.
Sat—5 miles at 7:00 pace.
Sun—20-26 miles at about 6:00 mile pace.

Chris follows the above schedule for 3-4 months and then does 3-4 months of casual, more enjoyable running at half to two-thirds the mileage. Chris enjoys backpacking, mountain climbing and cross country skiing—not to improve the running but to enjoy life and to avoid becoming a slave to the running.

Berka likes to eat ice cream and drink beer the night before a marathon. He eats only small amounts of meat and lots of fresh fruit.

I now enjoy taking a day off from running once every week or two—it refreshes the body and spirit. I usually start out each run at a pace I intend to continue—I don't like to start out slowly to "warmup" as I find it just makes me feel sluggish.

Running Philosophy: *Running is an opportunity to take time to enjoy and observe things in the outside world that we are usually isolated from or too distracted to notice.*

Racing Philosophy: *Racing is an opportunity to gather together all of one's energies and find out about them in a big narcissistic burst.*

JOHN BRAMLEY

One of a new line of unheralded runners who suddenly produce excellent marathon times, Bramley's improvement is due to hard work and perseverance.

JOHN ANDERSON BRAMLEY: Denver, Colorado. 5'6½", 135. Born March 17, 1954 in Denver, Colorado. Currently unemployed. John started competing and road racing at age 16. He plans to continue as long as he enjoys it and it gives him satisfaction. His favorite distance is the marathon. He has several advisors.

BEST MARKS: 3-mile, 14:35(76); 6-mile, 29:55(76); Roads: 5M, 25:03(76); 15k, 48:51(77); 10M, 51:15(76); 15M, 1:17:20(77); 25k, 1:22:43(77); 20M, 1:43:15(77); Marathon, 2:14:46(77).

TRAINING: John runs twice a day year-round. Morning runs are around 8-10AM and then again at 3-5PM. His longest ever run has been the marathons and a practice run of 23 miles. When he is training for the marathon, John likes to run a shorter race every week or two.
Mon—AM, 8-9 miles @ 6:30-7:00 or faster if feeling good. PM, 12-13 miles @ 6:00 pace or faster.
Tues—AM, 8-9 miles 6:30-7:00. PM, Jog 2 miles to park, 8-10 x 3min. hard runs, 5-6 miles warmdown; total 11 miles.
Wed—AM, 8-9 miles same. PM, 12-13 miles 6:00 pace or faster.
Thurs—AM, 8-9 miles same. PM, Jog 2-3 miles to dirt track. 20x440 or 10x880 with 440 jog recovery. 5-mile warmdown.
Fri—AM, 8-9 miles same. PM, 11-12 miles 6:00 pace.
Sat/Sun racing situation on either day—still at least 5 miles in the morning or evening of the race day. The other day is a long morning run of 15-20 miles and an afternoon run of 5 miles. This is the schedule 5 weeks prior to a marathon. Otherwise, he runs mainly overdistance above 100 miles a week. 8-10 weeks before a marathon, the overdistance increases leading into the above routine. John does cross country and downhill skiing in the winter months. If he is injured he swims. He uses the carbohydrate loading diet prior to a marathon.

As far as I am concerned there are no secret training techniques—the object to success is just doing the distance—especially in the marathon. I feel that from now on I will have to increase my mileage to 150-160 miles per week. The marathon is becoming extremely competitive and those that can handle more mileage will run better.

First—I enjoy it immensely (even though there are the tough days) but it's all worth it and so satisfying after completing an exhausting interval or distance workout and knowing I have accomplished something a lot of other people don't or can't accomplish and also realizing I am doing something so good for my body—for if you don't have your health you can't do anything. Secondly, of course, I continue running because I have progressed so well the last 2½ years and I know I have tremendous potential for the future. I have gained so much insight as an individual by being involved in running and at this time of my life there is nothing that makes me happier or gives me so much security than my running.

JOHN BRENNAND

One of the countries top Masters runners, Brennard started road racing at the late age of 27. He has successfully blended his running with his lifestyle, and has become a leading figure in the AAU hierarchy. Evidence of John's talent was his qualification for the Olympic Trials in 1972 at age 37.

JOHN BRENNAND: Santa Barbara, Calif. 5'9", 143. Born September 15, 1935 in El Paso, Texas. Occupation: Engineer working 40 hours per week. Married with two sons and one daughter. John started competing at age 27 on the roads. He plans to continue indefinitely. His favorite distance is 20-30k and he has no coach.

BEST MARKS: (Double times are before and after turning 40): Mile, 4:29(74); 1500m, 4:08(74); 1500, 4:15.9(78 Indoors); 25k, 1:26:50(77); 30k, 1:44:50(77); Marathon, 2:28:33(71) and 2:33:07(77); 2-mile, 9:30(74); 10,000m, 32:11(74) and 32:23(77).

TRAINING: John trains once a day, usually at noon, totalling 50-70 miles per week. On Sundays he does a long run of 16-20 miles. His longest run is 31 miles and he prefers to race once a month.

Mon—8 miles @ 7:00 pace.
Tues—10 miles @ 7:00 pace.
Wed—9 miles @ 6:30 pace.
Thurs—10 miles @ 7:00 pace.
Fri—Sometimes a few medium-effort miles during a 10 miler.
Sat—10 miles at 6:30-7:00 pace.
Sun—16-20 miles at 7:00 pace.
Sometimes before important races John will run a few mile repeats @ 5:30 pace with plenty of rest. He tapers his mileage to 40-50 prior to the race. He does a little stretching to supplement his running.

LEE FIDLER

Fidler's career demonstrates well that, in many cases, longevity is the key to good times.

LELAND WILLIS FIDLER, II: Stone Mountain, Georgia. 6'0", 150. Born March 21, 1949 in Baton Rouge, Louisiana. Occupation: Buyer for sports center, working 40 hrs/wk. Married. Lee started competing at age 15 and road racing at 20. He plans to continue indefinitely. His favorite distance is 10 miles. He is mostly self-coached but sometimes gets advice from his college coach.

BEST MARKS: 440, 56.0(72); 880, 2:04(76); mile, 4:17.0(71); 2-mile, 9:05(71); 3-mile, 13:59.7(71,77); 6-mile, 29:00(76). Roads: 5M, 23:16(76); 10M, 49:58(76); 15m, 1:14:43(76); One Hour, 11 miles 1081yds.(71); marathon, 2:16:51(75).

TRAINING: Lee runs twice a day 6 days per week and once the other day. He has not missed a day since May 15th, 1971. His longest ever run is 28 miles. He prefers to race every other week.
Mon—AM, 10 miles. PM, 5 miles.
Tues—AM, 10 miles. PM, 7 miles.
Wed—AM, 9 miles. PM, 10 miles fartlek or hill reps or a run at race pace.
Thurs—AM, 10 miles. PM, 5 miles.
Fri—AM, 10 miles. PM, 7 miles.
Sat—AM, 10 miles. PM, 5 miles.
Sun—AM, 20-24 miles. Lee's pace is dictated by the way he feels. His pace is between 5:16 and 7:00 per mile. The slower days are Monday and Thursday. Sunday is usually around 6:30 pace.

My training cycles are usually more intense in the spring and fall. During these periods I run more races. I usually point for a marathon in December, one in the spring, and the Peachtree Road Race on July 4th. July, August, January and February are less intense. I do only long and short distance runs. . . I stretch briefly before both runs; at the end of the day's running I stretch thoroughly for 15-20 minutes. I also do bent knee sit-ups and push-ups.

Lee does carbohydrate loading before marathons. He feels that consistency is one of his most effective training techniques.

I run for a number of reasons. The primary reason for my running is the drive toward perfection. I am motivated by the desire to be the best that I can be. I feel that I'll never know the best that I can be until my peak years of running have passed. Some people prefer to sit back and speculate about how much better athletes they could have been if they had sacrificed. I want to eliminate these doubts in my life. I can empathize with Don Quixote in the Man of La Mancha as he sings about dreaming the impossible dream and reaching for the unreachable star. The ultimate race will never be run. No matter how fast I run, I try to run faster.

Another reason for running is the people that I meet. Through running I have made friends across the country. Many races have become not only competitive events, but also reunions where old friends gather.

I also run for the travel. I have traveled throughout the country going to races. I have seen many places that I might have missed otherwise.

To someone who does not run I cannot rationalize the sacrifices that I have made to be a road runner.

TOM FLEMING

Hyper-consistent Tom Fleming is proof that good road racers come in all shapes and sizes. Led the 1979 Boston race through 15 miles, setting a torrid pace, yet still hung on for a near-PR 2:12:56.

TOM FLEMING: Bloomfield, New Jersey. 6'0", 154. Born July 23, 1951 at Long Branch, New Jersey. Running store owner working 40 hours per week. Married. Tom started competing and road racing at age 17. He plans to continue competitive road racing for many years to come. His favorite distance is 30k and he doesn't have a coach.

BEST MARKS: 1500m, 3:51.6, 2-mile, 8:41.6; 3 mile, 13:41.4; Road: 15k, 45:48; 20k, 1:00:55; 25k, 1:17:22; 30k, 1:30:58; marathon, 2:12:05(75).

TRAINING: Tom's longest training run was 35 miles; he prefers to race every two weeks. He has been doing the following routine for six years.

Mon—AM, 10 miles at 7:00 pace. PM, 10 miles @ 6:00 pace.
Tues—AM, 10 miles @ 7:00 pace. PM, 14 miles @ 6:00 pace.
Wed—AM, 10 miles @ 7:00 pace. PM, 10 miles hard fartlek.
Thurs—AM, 10 miles @ 7:00 pace. PM, 10 miles @ 7:00 pace.
Fri—AM, 10 miles @ 7:00 pace. PM, 14 miles @ 6:00 pace.
Sat—AM, 10 miles @ 7:00 pace. PM, 10 miles @ 7:00 pace.
Sun—long run 213 miles or race.
   Tom's training is. . . *always the same; some people can't believe how boring the whole routine is, but I have had success so I will keep it the same.*
   Right now, my main motivation for running is: 1. I want to be the best marathon runner I possibly can be and 2. I like all the great trips I get around the world for nothing—all I have to do is run, and I really love to run.

JEFF GALLOWAY

Jeff possesses incredible discipline, the ability to pace himself well, and thus get the most from his talent. Competed in the 10,000-meters in the 1972 Olympic Games.

JEFF GALLOWAY: Atlanta, Georgia. 5'11", 137. Born July 12, 1945 in Raleigh, North Carolina. Occupation: Phidippides owner, working 50 hrs/wk. Married. Started running at 14 and road racing at 19. Plans to continue indefinitely. Favorite distance is 10-20 miles.

BEST MARKS: 2-mile, 8:32(72); 5k, 13:41(72); 6-mile, 27:21(73); Marathon: 2:18:36(76).

TRAINING: Jeff runs twice a day year round except for one long run on Sundays. He runs at 8AM and 5-7PM. His longest ever run is 35 miles. He prefers to race every 2-3 weeks.
Mon—AM, 10 miles easy. PM, 10 miles easy.
Tues—AM, 10 miles easy. PM, 8 miles hill fartlek.
Wed—AM, 10 miles easy. PM, easy 10 miles.
Thurs—AM, 10 miles easy. PM, 6-8x1 mile @ 4:45 w/440 jog.
Fri—AM, 10 miles easy. PM, 10 miles easy.
Sat—AM, 10 miles easy. PM, race or pace effort at 6-8 miles.
Sun—AM, 20 miles.
Jeff does two six month cycles a year of the following phases: *Building phase:* 3 months easy distance with one hard run per week @ 160-180 miles per week. *Transition phase:* 2 months, 2 hard days/week (hill fartlek and a hard run) @ 140 miles a week. *Competitive phase:* 1 month 3 hard days/week with fartlek and intervals @ 110-120 miles per week. Jeff does stretching exercises. Over the years, his diet has come to include more fruits, vegetables and natural grains and cereals.

Special Training: *I've patterned my fartlek after some European training methods. I've developed an "interval-fartlek" that I think is effective for track racing.*

I really enjoy the quiet, still time to myself. It helps me touch some inner resources unreachable by other methods. The physical feeling of being fit is addicting. It gives me a feeling of excellence that carries over into other work and into my contacts with others.

DWAYNE HARMS

Peanut is typical of today's road racer: long-lived, experienced on the track, and totally involved with the sport. He is the prime mover behind the Aggie Running Club.

DWAYNE "PEANUT" HARMS. Mt. View, CA. 5'10¾", 134. Born May 27, 1951 in Richmond, CA. Coach working 50 hours per week. Started competing at age 20 and road racing at 22. His favorite distance is 10 miles. Harms is self-coached.

BEST MARKS: 440, 49.2r(72); 800m, 1:50.7(72); mile, 4:07.4(78); 2-mile, 8:51(77); 3-mile, 13:51(74); 6-mile, 29:29(77); 10-mile, 49:18(76); 25k, 1:22(78); marathon, 2:38(78); 10k, 29:58(78).

TRAINING: Dwayne trains, *once per day when not serious, 6 months per year; 2x a day for 3 months; other 3 months 3x, I'm really kind of lackadasical (relaxed).* His longest ever run is 29 miles and he prefers to race 2x a month when fit.

Mon—AM, 4-5 miles. PM, long fartlek (10 miles) or long intervals on track (rarely).
Tues—AM, 6-8 miles. PM, same.
Wed—AM, short speed work total 6-8 miles. PM, 6-8.
Thurs—PM, same as Tuesday.
Fri—One run of 10 miles with some pickups or hills.
Sat—4-6 miles AM, and repeat PM.
Sun—Long run, 1 hour, 30 minutes plus.

Training Cycles: *Training cycles are dependent upon when competitions are. In preparing for a top flight competition I race less and build more.*

Supplemental Exercises: *I usually do 5-10 minutes of stretching prior to running and stretching and jacuzzi afterwards.*

Special Diet: *No, I have a primarily vegetarian nutritional routine. Don't really believe in carbo loading.*

Training Techniques: *Self coach by doing hill charges until I forget where I parked my car.*

CARL HATFIELD

"Long-lived," is Carl Hatfield. He has been very consistent in the upper levels of American road racing for the past decade.

CARL EDWARD HATFIELD: Philippi, West Virginia. 5'8½", 136. Born May 5, 1947 in Matewan, West Virginia. Occupation: College Staff, Director of Student Activities, working 30-50 hours/week. Married with a 6-year-old son. Carl started competing at age 17 and road racing at age 23. He plans to continue until 1980. His favorite distance is 10,000m road or cross country.

BEST MARKS: 100y, 11.9(1967); 220Y, 24.1(67); 440y, 51.9(70); 880, 1:57.1(68); mile, 4:07r(68); 2-mile, 8:46i(71); 3-mile, 13:49.6(72); 10,000m, 29:37(73); Roads: 10k, 30:12(71); 15k, 47:32(77); 10M 49:07(74); 20k, 1:20:31; 15M, 1:16:21(77); 25k, 1:18:31(76); Marathon, 2:17:26(76).

TRAINING: Carl usually runs twice a day 6 days a week and once on the other day, 12 months a year. His longest run has been the marathon and longest training run was 22 miles. He prefers to race once every two weeks.
Mon—AM, 8 miles at 7½ pace. PM, 12 miles at 7:00 pace.
Tues—AM, 4 miles at 7:00 pace. PM, 14 miles of fartlek with either 3 x mile at 4:55, or 6 x 440(70) and 6 x 880(2:25).
Wed—AM, rest. PM, 8 miles at 7:00 pace.
Thurs—AM, 8 miles at 7:00 pace. PM, 12 miles @ 6:30 pace with pickup at end.
Fri—AM, 8 miles. PM, 4-8 miles easy if race if not then 12 miles easy.
Sat—AM, race; or 4-8 miles @ 7:00. PM, race or 12 miles at 7:00.
Sun—AM, race; or 8 miles at 8:00 pace. PM, 16-18 miles at 6:30 pace.
This is 90-110 miles per week but Carl usually misses one or more of the morning runs of 8 miles because he likes to stay up late and read.
At present I run two major marathons—Boston in the spring and New York in the fall—and I generally point toward

these two races by starting 6-8 weeks beforehand and build up by running the 16-18 miles loop on time once or twice a week. The training gets more intense and faster as the race approaches and then I ease off starting about 5 days before the race.

Carl does about 5 minutes of stretching exercise before and after each workout. In the summer he swims and canoes; in the winter he does some cross country skiing. He uses carbohydrate-loading before marathons. Before shorter races he avoids meat and sticks to a carbohydrate meal the night before.

I live in an area of many hills and all my loops involve going up and down these hills. On the days when I do my fartlek of 8-14 miles, I do intervals of 440-1 mile in length both up and down hills. I feel this training in the hills makes me especially effective on a hilly course or one with hills situated as the hills are in Boston.

I sometimes wonder if I could put my time to better use by reading or learning to play the guitar or getting to know my son better. But I love competition, and the excitement of racing, running a faster time or proving I can conquer a certain type of course. . . . But the major reason I continue is the companionship and common interest that is shared. . . I consider myself a better person for having been in running and track for nine years. There is something that is pure, strong about running. Society as we know it today falls short of such experiences. Also, running is a form of self-expression. I try to prove that I can accomplish something.

HAL HIGDON

Hal has been a model for the "continuing runner." A member of several international teams, Higdon has continued to race at a serious level, and to write about his experiences doing it, for the past 30 years.

HAL HIGDON: Michigan City, Indiana. 5'10", 140. Born June 17. 1931 in Chicago. Hal is a writer working 20-60 hours per week. He is married with 3 children. He started competing at 15 and road racing at 21. He plans to continue forever. His favorite distance is the 3000m steeplechase.

BEST MARKS:

100y, 11.1; 220, 24.5; 440, 52.2(54); 880, 1:59.8(54); mile, 4:13.6(57); 2-mile, 9:15(59); 3-mile, 14:10(65); 5,000m, 14:43.6(56); 14:59.8(72); SC, 9:13.8(58).

Roads:

15k, 47.05(75); 10m, 51.30(75); 30k, 1:40.72(73); marathon, 2:21.55(64); 2:34.37(77).

TRAINING: Hal usually trains once a day but occassionally twice for certain periods. He trains at all times of the day and night depending on his schedule. His longest ever run is 31 miles in a workout but he prefers a maximum of 17-18. He likes to race once a week in peak season and less often in the off-season.

Mon—7 miles gentle cross country.
Tues—Early PM, 2 miles easy fartlek, late PM, 5 miles cross country fast pace.
Wed—AM, 6.5 miles road, easy. PM, 10 miles, beach and road, easy.
Thurs—AM, 3 miles road, easy. PM, 10 miles cross country, push at end.
Fri—AM, 2.5 miles, beach, easy, PM, 10 miles road & cross country.
Sat—AM, 2 miles easy then hard. PM, 8 miles, good pace.
Sun—AM, 17 miles, gentle pace. PM, 3 miles easy, golf course.

Training cycles: *Sometimes when very bust, or less motivated, I may only run a few miles a day. Other times whole pointing for major races I will increase the intensity, maybe even add some track work which I normally don't do. But basically the pattern is the same, the intensity(speed or distance) varying from month to month.*

Supplementary exercise: *I try to do some stretching before or during most runs; I don't always succeed. During certain off seasons I do some weight lifting, but low weights and relatively few reps.*

Diet: *I eat less meat now than I did in the past and like most others, have more carbohydrates in my normal meal pattern. I avoid most fatty foods. I have been away from the marathon for five years and only now have begun to experiment with carbohydrate loading for that race. I'm still working our my modification, but it differs from the usual pattern.*

Unique or Unusual training techniques: *I do a lot of my training over varied terrain, both road and cross country. And the terrain includes hills and different footing. Because of this I am forced into a varied pace, so I do workouts of this nature rather than interval work on the track. Runs on certain courses become fartlek runs because of the nature of the course, so this gives me great variety in my workout pattern.*

Running Philosophy: *One reason why I race intensively as a master is possibly because of unfulfillment during my younger years. I had good shots at the Olympic team in 56,60,64, but fell short. Two of those years I might have come closer except for injuries. I train much more intelligently now and seem to be able to limit injuries because I have a better sense of my capabilities. Also, I have a better sense of my motivational limitations and do not either train or race intensively year after year. Often I will have a very intense period of competition followed by a period of either fun running or no competition. I'll take a year off. This permits me to come back with greater zest the following season. I also have managed to balance my work and running along with my family life. In fact, I have all sorts of rationalizations as to why I need to both run and race. But basically it comes back to the fact that I enjoy it. And I suppose it also gets back to the fact that we enjoy doing what we do well.*

KAJ JOHANSEN

Kaj demonstrates that factors like an intense professional life, non-typical physical dimensions, and lack of leg speed do not prohibit a person from being a successful road racer.

KAJ JOHANSEN: San Diego, California. 6'5", 190. Born March 6, 1945 in Astonia, Oregon. Kaj is a surgeon working 120 hours a week. Married with a 5-year-old daughter. He started road racing at 27 and had previously competed at race walking (16) and rowing (19). He plans to continue indefinitely. His favorite distance is 15 miles and up. He is advised by Tom Bache and Peter Fredriksson.

BEST MARKS: Mile, 5:01; 6-mile, 32:10(75); 10k, 33:02(74); 15k, 50:30(73); 10M, 54:10(75); 20k, 68:40(75); 25k, 1:26:27(75); marathon, 2:27:12(74); 50k, 2:57(74); one hour, 11 miles 145 yds(75).

TRAINING: During grad school, Kaj trained twice daily except once on Sunday throughout the year, but experienced no major guilt over missing a workout. Currently trains once a day and twice on Sundays. His longest ever race was 34 miles on the track. He prefers to race every other week for distances less than 20k and once a month for 20k-20 miles. Marathon frequency is one each 3-4 months. Monday through Saturday—All these workouts are currently the same: AM, 11 miles at 6:30 pace. PM, 11 miles at 6:30 pace, alternating with single workouts of 11 miles at 6:30 pace. Therefore a hard/easy approach.

Previously, when I was not in my surgical residency, I did 11 miles in the morning and after noon 15 miles. From 1973-1975, I averaged about 140 miles a week and was essentially never injured. This explains how a 5:00 miler can run 2:27 and win the U.S. 50k Championship.

On Sunday AM, a two hour hard race pace type run with as many hills as possible is done with a group of 2:20 level marathoners (Camp, Fredriksson, Akiyama, Kastischke, Hunt, etc.). In the afternoon he runs 10 miles at 6:00 pace. His marathon preparation involves a 3-month cycle using the above schedule for 2 months and increasing hills, fartlek and other higher quality work the last month. He does no supplementary exercises currently, though he recognizes a certain need to do some torso/shoulder exercises.

I specifically avoid stretching exercises, believing that they don't increase speed or endurance and do not mitigate against injuries. I'm quite convinced by the physiological data and by my own experience in 13 of 15 marathons that carbohydrate loading prior to marathons is effective. I eat everything put in front of me, drink 2 six packs of beer a week and take no vitamins or supplements. I don't think interval training plays a significant role in marathon training and in fact is probably potentially destructive, both emotionally and in terms of risking injuries. 2) It's very productive to train with other runners, especially runners faster than oneself.

I race for ego-enhancing reasons: it's something I'm good at, and the return for effort expended is significant. I run for obscure, aristotelian reasons: my professional life as an academic surgeon is so cerebral, rarefied, and intricate, that I require a sort of antidote in the form of a simple outdoor motor skill that I do well and makes me feel good physically. Thus, I would continue running even if I could never race anymore.

DON KARDONG

Don may be called the Court Jester of the running movement. His irreverent attitude keeps him loose, and his many other outside interests are, in fact, one reason for his running success—he is not defined solely by his running. High-point of his career thus far has been his 4th place finish in the 1976 Montreal Olympic marathon, 3 seconds out of 3rd place.

DONALD FRANKLIN KARDONG: Spokane, Washington. 6'3", 150. Born December 22, 1948 in Kirkland, Washington. Occupation: entrepreneur. Don is single and does not admit to any descendents. He started competing at 15 and road racing about the same age. He plans to continue road racing, "until the road is clearly the victor." His favorite distance is one light-year and his coach/advisor is Greg Brock.

BEST MARKS: Mile, 4:01.9(74); 2-mile, 8:32.6(72); 3-mile, 12:57.6(74); 6-mile, somewhere around 28:00. marathon, 2:11:16(76).

TRAINING: *Basically, twice a day, year-round, at virtually any time of day or night, sometimes only once a day, sometimes not at all, but always (usually) fifteen miles a day, except when there is something more tempting to do, like watching the Flintstones or something.*

His longest ever run was 26 miles 385 yards and he prefers to race every two weeks.

Mon—AM, 10 miles @ 6:23 pace. PM, 10 miles @ 6:07 pace.
Tues—AM, 15 miles @ 6:18 pace. PM, nothing.
Wed—AM, 5 miles @ 6:31 pace. PM, 20x315 yards on the grass or in the dirt @ a pick-me-up pace with once around the nearby bush or wading pool for recovery.
Thurs—AM, 10 miles @ 6:04 pace. PM, 5 miles @ 6:16 pace.
Fri—AM, 10 miles @ 6:01 pace. PM, 5 miles @ 5:54 pace.
Sat—AM or PM, 15 miles @ 6:13 pace.
Sun—PM, 19 miles @ 6:10 pace.

Training Cycles: *In winter, I run LSD, because the streets are icy and the process of natural selection has eliminated runners who tend to do interval work on icy streets. Spring and fall I do two interval workouts a week. I can't remember what I do in the summer.*

Don does Sheehan's magic six for stretching. He staunchly defends his diet of Fruit Loops, beer and pizza and feels it has the right of endorsement as much as some of the exotic health food routines of people who have run much slower marathon times. Running/Racing philosophy:

To be a better runner,
To be the very best,
Run more and more and more and more,
But less, and less, and less.

JACK LEYDIG

"Bonus Jack" is another example of the total running lifestyle. *Eminence Gris of the West Valley Track Club, editor of the Nor-Cal Running Review, owner of Jack's Athletic Supply* . . . *running is Leydig's business as well as his hobby.*

JACK LEYDIG. San Mateo (West Valley Track Club). 5'11½", 145. Born January 14, 1944, in San Francisco, CA. Self-employed sporting goods salesman working 10-30 hours per week. Married. Started competing at 16 and road racing at 18. Jack plans to continue competitively until he *keels over from malnutrition, disease, or heart failure.* His favorite distance is 10-20k and he is self-coached.

BEST MARKS: 440; 53.5(64); 880, 1:48.1(63); mile, 4:16.5(66); 2-mile, 9:18.5(66); 10k, 30:50(roads-71); Hour, 11 miles 959 yards(76); 30k, 1:39:00(72); marathon, 2:25:15(72).

TRAINING: Jack trains, *once per day, 5-7 days per week, all year round; if I have time I'll try and get 2-3 morning runs in per week . . . normally runs are in late afternoon.* Jack has covered 32 miles both in a race and in a practice. He prefers to race 2-3 times per month.

Jack tries to follow a modified Lydiard system ideally:
Base Period (3-4 months)
Mon—PM, 8-10 miles @ 6:00-15. Tues—PM, 12-15M @ 6:10-20. Wed—PM, 10M; fartlek. Thurs—PM, 12-15M @ 6:10-6:20. Fri—PM, 8M @ 6:30 if racing Saturday or 10-mile fartlek. Sat—AM, race (not longer than 25k if racing). Sun—AM, 16-22M @ 6:30-7:00.

Hill Period (6-8 Wks)
Mon—AM, 8-10 miles fartlek/hills. Tues—AM, 5-6M easy; PM, hill bounding/strides. Wed—10-12M steady 6:30. Thurs—same as Tues. Fri—PM, 10M fartlek/hills or 8M easy if racing Saturday. Sat—AM, race (20k max if racing). Sun—AM, 18-2M F 6:30-7:00.

Speed & Intervals (6-8 Wks)
Mon—8-10M @ 6:20. Tues—5-10k "time trial" at 90%.
Wed—AM, 6-7M easy; PM, 10M @ 6:00. Thurs—PM, repeat
880s or miles; Fri—AM, 8M easy if race Saturday. Sat—race
(20k max). Sun—AM, 18-22M @ 6:15-20 (strides before and
after all hard effort days).

Training Cycles: *If I'm trying to peak for a particular
race(s) or season, I'll increase my intensity over the 3-4 months
preceding that period, then will cut back in volume when I
want to race well and increase my intensity. I generally try to
point for one good marathon a year, if I'm not injured.*

Supplementary exercise: *I try to stretch 5-10 minutes after
each workout; I do some light weight training when I have
time, but probably not as much as I should.*

Special Diet: *I used to eat a light breakfast before competition, but I don't anymore. I tried carbo-loading once without
too much success, but think that the depletion phase may
have wiped me out. I still do carbo load before longer runs
but without the depletion phase. Other than that, my diet
stays pretty much the same year around . . . I try to get a
well-balanced diet and still eat some junk food. I take vitamin
and protein supplements and precautionary measures.*

Training Techniques: *I have had pretty good success with
low mileage (lack of time to train). If I can't get in high
mileage for a good base then I run most of my workouts
fairly hard (at 6:00 or better) with an increase in pace over
the last few miles . . . this gets me in the habit of auto-
matically increasing my tempo in a race towards the end,
much longer from the finish then would be considered
'normal'. I can race fairly well on 45-60 miles per week with
very few long runs . . . at distances up to about 15 miles.*

Why Run: *I run because (1) It's something I do well and
still feel I can improve at; (2) It's good for my head and my
body . . . it's a 'release' from the tensions of everyday life and
I feel like it's obviously prolonging my life . . . or at least making
it more enjoyable; (3) Most everything I do is tied in with
running (including my jobs and hobby . . . NorCal Running
Review) and so it's hard not to compete. I would run even if
I couldn't race, just to maintain fitness, but I much prefer to
test myself with either races or time trials.*

HERB LINDSAY

Herb made a tremendous breakthrough on the roads in 1979, with important wins in the Lynchburg 10k in American Record time, and at the Diet Pepsi 10k, where he beat all of his major rivals. This immensely strong athlete was named Road Racer of the Year for 1979 by Track & Field News.

HERBERT DONALD LINDSAY. Boulder, Colorado. 5-9, 145. Born November 12, 1954 in Grand Rapids, Mich. Works in retail sporting goods sales 25-30 hours per week. Married. Started competing at age 15, road racing at 16. Plans to continue racing over his running lifetime. Lindsay has no favorite racing distance.

BEST MARKS: 440, 52.0(72); 880, 1:54.8(75); Mile (relay indoors), 3:59.1(76); 2-mile, 8:38(i—75); 5k, 13:41(79); 10k, 28:21(79); 15k, 43:50(79); 10-mile, 47:02 AR(79).

TRAINING: Herb generally runs twice a day, six days per week, with the 7th day being one long run of approximately 20 miles.

In general, morning runs follow this schedule: up @ 5:50, out the door by 6:00. Run with wife Terry for the first 3-4 miles at a very easy pace, after which she head for home and I continue for another 3-4 miles. (Distance depends on the weather, how I feel, the amount of sleep I had the night before.) Generally, the morning run M-F consists of 50-70 minutes of activity. I sometimes do a one-to-two mile pick-up on the morning run. But this depends again on how I am feeling. I'm big on bio-feedback: One advantage to being a post-collegiate distance runner is not having to listen to coaches' commands—you can listen to your own body.

In addition, I make it a point to run West—towards the mountains and uphill—every day. I often make this my pickup mile, midway through the AM run.

Mon—PM, One hour run or 10 miles, whichever comes first. Tues—PM, fartlek on city streets and/or city mountain park trails; or repeat laps around the intramural football field—2x3 laps, 2x2 laps, 3x1 lap. *These workouts vary; I like to mix 'em up.*

Wed—PM, Trail run or long road run of 60 to 80 minutes. Thurs—PM, *Maybe* another Tuesday type workout; or a timed run on the road for 20-25-30 minutes; or alternating 2:30 minutes of "effort" running on the roads with easy 2:30 recovery, times 4-5; or "shadow racing," a form of fartlek run alone.

Other variations on hard day workouts (which generally fall on Tues-Thurs): Hill climbing up an 800+ meter uphill road, striding the first part and working hard at maintaining after grade steepens. Do 4-times up and down. This is called the "Boomerang" workout after the shape of the road, or the "Arbo" after Guy Arbogast who "is tough to beat on it."

Fri—PM, Long run of an hour to 75 minutes, or more if feeling good; less if feeling poorly.

Sat—AM, Half-hour run, longer and later than M-F runs. PM, One hour run.

Sun—1½-2 hour run in AM. Sometimes 4-5 mile run in PM with Terry, very easy.

Herb prefers to race within a framework of heavy and light racing months; i.e., a heavy month will have him racing every weekend or every other; a light months will be two races. September 1979 was heavy, with 4-5 races; December 1979 was light with only one race. Race schedule depends on bio-feedback. *Listen to your body to tell you when to race, when to rest.*

Training Cycles: *Training intensity is dependent on the importance of the event—I generally work harder and rest more for the more important events, such as national championships, 3-4 times per year.*

Supplementary Exercises: *Stretching daily after the AM run and after the PM run—after dinner while watching TV, listening to the stereo, reading, etc.*

Special Diet: *No special diet—I've recently lost weight, however, by cutting back on total calorie intake.*

Running Philosophy: *Running has provided me with opportunities which would not have been possible if I was not involved in the sport, such as varied travel experiences, the chance to work with people, meet new people, develop my own skills with people, meet professional people for future career opportunities. I enjoy the challenge of working toward self-defined goals. I challenge myself to succeed.*

ANGEL MARTINEZ

How to balance business and family commitments with the time required for road racing? Like many road racers, Angel is struggling with this dilemma.

ANGEL RAMON MARTINEZ: Mt. View, CA. 5'11", 150. Born May 4, 1955, in Camaguey, Cuba. Retail store manager working 50+ hours a week. Started competing at 14 and road racing at 15. He plans to continue racing until he doesn't enjoy it. Favorite distance is 8-15 miles.

BEST MARKS: 440, 51.8(73); 800m, 1:59.8(73); mile, 4:13.1(76); 2-mile, 8:56.3(76); 5,000, 14:21(78); 10,000, 29:38(78); 25k, 1:20:41(78); marathon, 2:22:8(78).

TRAINING: Angel trains once per day, 5-6 days per week, averaging 8-10 miles at sub-6:00 pace. Angel prefers running in the afternoon and trains 10-11 months of year. His longest ever run is a marathon. Racing preference is every 2-3 weeks during racing months.

I don't follow a particular schedule—my work week doesn't afford the luxury. So, I usually wind up running as I feel. If I feel like running hard 5:30-6:00, I do. If not, I don't. More often than not my runs are at that pace. Sometimes, I don't run for weeks.

Training Cycles: *Summer usually allows me more time to train. So summers are usually pretty intense. Also, there is no pollution in the summer, most track seasons are usually ruined by hay fever.*

Supplementary Exercise: *Lots of lower arm flexions with 16 oz. beer mug in hand. Also do lots of gymnastics type exercises for flexibility. Do Bowerman conversions (i.e., vertical miles) count.*

Diet: *Lots of Cuban food.*

Training Technique: *I frequently run very fast road workouts (5:00 pace) for as long as I can last. This has become known as the "Martinez Kamakazi Method" among my Aggie RC teammates.*

KEN MOORE

Moore is a two-time Olympian, and achieved a 4th-place finish in the 1972 Munich marathon. An author and magazine writer, Moore articulates in his writings the feelings of serious runners. Perhaps a made runner more than a born one, Kenny has made his body respond to the dictates of his intellect.

KENNETH C. MOORE: Eugene, Oregon. 6', 144. Born December 1, 1943 in Portland, Oregon. Ken is a journalist and respondent to questionnaires working between 0 and 100 hours per week. Ken is unmarried presently but, *best running was done with the help of a splendid wife.* He plans to continue competitive road racing indefinitely. His favorite distance is the half-marathon. His coach/advisor is William J. Bowerman.

BEST MARKS: 100y, 11.2(69); 220, 24.8(64); 440, 52.0(64); 880, 1:55.0(67); 1500m, 3:47.2(72); mile, 4:03.2(72); 2-mile, 8:43.2i(65); 3-mile, 13:18.4(71); 5000m, 13:44.0(72); 10,000m, 28:47(70); marathon, 2:11:36(70).

TRAINING: Ken trains at 9AM and 3PM 6 days per week and one long run on the 7th day beginning in late AM. His longest ever run is 43 miles. Preferred racing frequency is once a month and dwindling. Ken's easy days are a 5½ - 8 mile jog in the morning and sometimes an easy three mile jog in the afternoon on Pre's Trail. The following workouts were done prior to the 1978 New York Marathon.

Sun—Sept. 25—write Bill Rodgers profile.
Mon—Jog 6 miles.
Tues—Brainstorm Eric Heiden, embellish notes,—run 6 x mile on Pre's Trail in 4:40-4:44.
Wed—Easy day and garden work.
Thurs—Easy day.
Fri—32-mile run.
Sat—Easy day.
Sun—Easy day.
Mon—6x330 on track on grass(last 6 45.5-46), easy 6 miles.

Tues—Easy day.
Wed—Easy day.
Thurs—6 x mile @ 4:40.
Fri—Easy day.
Sat—Easy day.
Sun—28-mile run.
Mon—Easy day.
Tues—Easy day.
Wed—3x660(1:42), 440(66), 330(48), 220(32), 110(15), jog 10 miles.
Thurs—Easy day.
Fri—Easy day.
Sat—6 x mile @4:36.
Sun—Easy day, fly to Washington D.C.
Mon—15 miles easy.
Tues—Easy day.
Wed—10 mile run, 1st five at 7:00 pace and second five at 5:00 pace.
Thurs—Easy day.
Fri—Easy day, go to New York.
Sat—Easy day.
Sun—New York City Marathon, 2:16:29. Ken did not run for the next 8 days but on the 27th of October won a pumpkin carving contest at Bob Newland's house.

Ken increases his training diligence and mileage (toward 100/wk) the 12 weeks prior to a marathon. He does between 15 and 20 pullups on easy days, or more if necessary to establish supremacy.

Training Techniques: *The emphatic nature of my hard and easy days, especially easy, is best for me, and probably best for all those runners who seem to get hurt or sick with regularity.*

Philosophy: *This must await a future tome—(ah, but Ted Brock has a view that is pertinent just now. "No matter what else it is," he said, "marathon training is fine post-marriage therapy.")*

JIM NUCCIO

Jim has been called one of the "new breed" of runners who specializes in road races. He prefers to race between 15 and 25 kilometers, and likes to race often and fast. A good road racer when healthy. He is also a gourmand.

JAMES EDWARD NUCCIO: Corte Madera, California. 5'9", 140. Born January 24, 1950 in Pasadena, California. Occupation: Real Estate Sales working 60 Hours/wk. Married, with one child. He started running at age 14 and road racing at 23. He plans to race quite a while longer.

BEST MARKS: 100y, 10.3(68); 440, 50.2(68); 880, 1:52.5(68); mile, 4:11.4(70); 2-mile, 8:56.8(72); 3-mile, 13:45.4(72); 6-mile, 28:25.1(72); 15K Track, 45:07(75); 10-miles, 48:25(75); 1 Hour, 12 miles 372 Yds.(76); 25K, 1:17:22(77).

TRAINING: Jim trains twice a day (except on Sunday) at 5AM and 4-5PM and 9AM on Sunday. His longest ever run is 26 miles 385 yds. He prefers to race once a month except during peak racing season when he will run successive weekends during a racing month. He finishes most workouts with 15x110 run at a 1-hard and 1-shakeup pace.
Mon—AM, 7 Plodding miles, 15x110. PM, 13 miles @ 6:00+ pace, 15x110.
Tues—AM, 5 plodding miles, 15x110. PM, 8 miles (5 hard, 3 fartlek w/440-660 efforts), 15x110.
Wed—AM, 7 plodding miles. PM, 14 miles @ 6:30 pace or faster, 15x110.
Thurs—AM, 12 miles faster than plod. PM, 8 miles (easy 5, 3 hard fartlek w/220-330 intervals), 15x110.
Fri—AM, 5 easy, 15x110. PM, 5 easy, 15x110.
Sat—AM, 7 plod. PM, 10 miles all out (4:50-5:00), 15x110.
Sun—AM, 21+ @ 6:45-7:00 pace, 15x110. This and the Wed. afternoon run are with other runners and are run at a comfortable pace for all.

This year I've experimented with a training cycle. Before a big race, I've been putting in 2 or 3 consecutive weeks of medium-paced distance, 155-160 miles per week; followed by 3 weeks of the above schedule with the target race at the end of the third week.

Of the organized sports I've been actively involved with (Baseball, Basketball, Football, Track), distance running offers the greatest amount of freedom—you're not dependent on 10 other clowns. You can train whenever, wherever and however you please, without the anxiety of possibly "hurting" the team. I also run so I can eat more.

BILL RODGERS

Bill dropped out of the running scene soon after college, but started running to work and back after his motorcycle was stolen. This crime paid, at least for American distance running. Rodgers races almost exclusively on the roads but has excellent track marks as well. His recent win in the New York Marathon establishes him as one of the all time great marathon runners.

WILLIAM HENRY RODGERS: Melrose, Mass. 5'8½", 128. Born December 23, 1947 in Hartford, Conn. Occupation: Businessman working about 40 hrs/wk. Married. Started running at age 16 and first ran on the roads at 18, though not seriously until age 25. Favorite distances are 2k to the marathon. Rodgers plans to compete indefinitely. Bill Squires, Greater Boston TC coach, is his advisor.

BEST MARKS: Track: 800, 2:01; mile, 4:18.8; 2-mile, 8:53.6; 3-mile, 13:25.4; 6-mile, 27:10; 10,000, 28:04.4; 15,000, 43:39.8, 10M, 46:35; 20k, 58:15; Hour, 12 miles 1,351 yds. road: 10k, 28:16; 15k, approx. 46 minutes; 20k. 60:20: 25k, 1:17:37; 30k, 1:29:04; marathon, 2:09:27(79).

TRAINING: Bill runs twice a day, seven days a week, the year round. His sessions are at 11:00 a.m. and 5:00 p.m. approximately. His longest run has been 32 miles. He prefers to race every 3 weeks or so.
Mon—AM, 9 miles at 6-6:30 pace. PM, 12 miles @ 6-6:30 pace.
Tues—Intervals on track: 6x440 and 6x880 at 70 sec. pace (10-12 miles).
Wed—12 miles @ 6-6:30 pace.
Thurs—12 miles @ 6-6:30 pace.
Fri—12 miles @ 6-6:30 pace.
Sat—12 miles @ 6-6:30 pace.
Sun—AM, 20 miles at 6-7:00 pace. PM, 5-10 miles @ 6-6:30 pace.

My training is generally similar year round, except I have usually used the summer as a low-key training

period—easier paced runs and very few track workouts. In the late summer, prior to my heaviest racing period (Sept-Oct), I increase my mileage. I do this in the 2 month period before any major competition, especially the marathon. I aim for 150 or more miles per week. Winter often cuts down the intensity (amount of miles and pace) at which I train.

Bill usually stretches after running and before races. He skips meat the day of and before competition. Before marathons he tries to increase his potassium intake by drinking fruit juices, ERG and eating tomatoes and bananas. He also takes some vitamins.

He believes in running through fields and woods to develop skill at running on uneven surfaces and the beneficial psychological effects gained from the environment.

I run for a variety of reasons though one of the primary, if not the primary reason is because I enjoy the physical movements of running which seems to help me feel better psycho-emotionally and physically. I like the natural and primitive aspects of running.

TONY SANDOVAL

Fourth in the 1976 Olympic Trials marathon, Tony is one of Frank Shorter's picks for the team in 1980, because of his great success with low mileage. When Sandoval has time to train (he is a medical student), many feel that his real talent for the marathon will emerge.

ANTHONY BENIGNO SANDOVAL: Los Alamos, New Mexico. 5'8", 115. Born May 19, 1954 at Santa Fe, New Mexico. Tony is a medical student. He started competing at age 16 and road racing at 17. He plans to continue road racing, *for as long as my skinny legs can take it.* His favorite distance for road racing is 5-15 miles. His coach/advisor is Marshall Clarke, formerly of Stanford.

BEST MARKS: Mile, 4:04(75); 2-mile, 8:47(76); 3-mile, 13:25(76); 5,000m, 13:50(76); 6-mile, 28:03(76); 10,000m, 28:53(76); Hr., 11M,1000y; mara, 2:10:20(79).

TRAINING: Tony usually runs twice a day. His longest ever run in training is 23 miles. He prefers to race every two to three weeks.

Tony is currently in the process of adjustment from the regimented demands and secure training schedules of his college career. He feels most of his success thus far in road races has been a by product of his cross country and track orientation from Stanford.

Tony's morning runs are usually 6-8 miles in 40-50 minutes unless he sleeps late, then it is 3-4 just to wake up. Afternoons, he does his serious road runs of from 4-20 miles. He likes to start easy and build, sometimes to as fast as 5:00 pace. He supplements this base training with short quick repeat work on a golf course and fartlek work. He always adds this prior to races as he feels more comfortable having done some quick work to "stretch out."

Tony does some light and basic weight work, situps and pushups and, most important, pullups. He eats little the day before a race and the day of the race. After racing he devours everything in sight.

Tony has very strong and special feelings about both his running experience and his collegiate track coach, Marshall Clarke. *Our talks often are evaluative rather than directive of my training. Yet, we do have a certain goal or basic circumstance that we work toward. You might say we carry on a "romance" from my days at Stanford. We are good friends and have insights into each others goals in athletics and in life.* It will be interesting to see if Tony can make the transition from college running through medical school and return to high class running with the zest and success of Don Kardong and Duncan Macdonald, other Stanford Alumni.

FRANK SHORTER

Some say Frank started it all. That road racing was the backwater of a very small bay before he caught the imagination of America in the 1972 Olympic marathon. Certainly, many of the runners in this book were inspired by that performance. And many of the thousands of today's joggers view him as a demi-god of the sport.

Today, Frank is shooting for his third Olympic Games. Unlike his first in 1972 and his second in 1976, he won't have to worry about supporting himself and his family while he trains, as his Frank Shorter Running Gear is booming. Now the man who dominated road racing through the mid-70s is fighting a harder struggle—to keep his body together in order that the powers of his mind can be directed towards the goal once again.

Below is reprinted Shorter's training program from 1973. Since then, when asked how he trains, Frank's answer has been, "The same as ever." It is the program which brought him success, and we hope, will do so again.

FRANK CHARLES SHORTER: Boulder, Colo. 5-10½, 135. Born Oct. 31, 1947 in Munich, West Germany. Lawyer and businessman, working 50 hours per week. Married, with one child. Began racing at age 15 in 1963. Self-coached.

BEST MARKS: 3000, 7:51.4 (72); 2M, 8:26.2i (71); 3M, 12:52.0 (74); 5000, 13:26.7 (77); 10k, 27:46.0 (75); Marathon, 2:10:30 (72).

TRAINING: Frank runs in the morning every day, 7-10 easy miles, at 6:30 to 7:00 pace.

Four days a week, during the afternoons, Shorter runs 15-20 miles at 6:00 pace or faster. The other three afternoons are given over to interval training, emphasizing fast repetitions with short recoveries. Frank has become famous for the brutality of his interval sessions. One example is 15 x 440 in 62-64, with a *50-yard* recovery jog. Another interval session used by Shorter is a variation on Ron Clarke's

50-60s: 50-yard sprint, followed by 60-yard jog, 50-yard sprint, 60-jog, and so on to exhaustion.

Shorter averages 120-160 miles per week, and he changes his training regimen very little over the course of a year.

CHUCK SMEAD

Smead is an example of an outstanding southern California prep athlete who has continued to run well in long races, particularly in the marathon and hill races.

CHUCK SMEAD: Santa Paula, California. 5'9", 140. Born August 4, 1951 in Ventura, California. Teacher working 40 hours a week. Married with one child. Chuck started competing at 13 and road racing at 17. He plans to continue indefinitely. His favorite distance is 15 to 20 miles and prefers uphill—the steeper the better.

BEST MARKS: 50y, 5.8(75); 220, 24.8(73); 440, 54.8(74); 880, 1:56.0(76); 1320, 3:01(77); Mile, 4:12(74); 2-mile, 8:53(77); 3-mile, 13:42(76); 6-mile, 28:28(73); 10k road, 29:24(78); 15k road, 46:02(77); 20k road, 1:01:28(76); 25k road, 1:19:20(74); 30k road, 1:37:10(71); marathon, 2:14:38(77); 50k road, 2:50:45—American Record.

TRAINING: Chuck trains twice daily at 6:00AM and 3:00PM every day but occasionally just runs one long run on a weekend day. His longest-ever run was 48 miles through mountains in 11 hours with extreme terrain. He prefers to race once every two weeks.

Mon—AM, 6 miles in 45-50 minutes. PM, track workout.
Tues—AM, Same as Mon. PM, 10-12 miles in 75 minutes.
Wed—AM, Same. PM, track workout.
Thurs—AM, Same, but sometimes 12 miles. PM, 10-12 miles in 75 minutes.
Fri—AM, Same. PM, 10-12 miles; or 15-20 mile mountain run usually above 5000'.
Sat—AM, 6-10 miles at 7:00 pace. PM, 5-mile warmup and 3-mile trial on track or race or one long mountain run.
Sun—Depends on Saturday. Do the reverse.

My training is always more intense in the summer because of no job pressures and location (altitude). I am always in my best shape in August.

Chuck supplements his running with 15-20 minutes of stretching each morning as well as doing pushups, pullups, situps and back exercises 3 times a week. He follows no special diet but makes sure his weight stays down. *I am actually a mountain runner. My strength is running uphill at altitude. I can also run the road races at high altitude better, compared to other runners at sea-level. I have run 2:23 at 6000', and 2:25 at 7,500'. I run because I enjoy it. I like the challenge of racing and trying to improve as much as possible. I just like the feeling of being in shape.*

RICK TRUJILLO

Trujillo is a man in harmony with his environment, an environment of his choosing. Rick is a runner.

RICHARD S. TRUJILLO: Ouray, Colorado. 6'1", 155. Born March 13, 1948 in Montrose, Colorado. Rick is a mining geologist and works 40 hours a week. Single. He started competing at 15 and road racing at 18. He plans to compete seriously only a few more years but running and occasionally racing indefinitely. His favorite distance is 10-15 miles (1-2 hours).

BEST MARKS: Mile, 4:06.2(68); 2-mile, 8:57.6(68); 10,000m, 29:32(68); Pikes Peak Marathon(26.8miles), 3:31(75).

TRAINING: From April through October, Rick trains once a day, Mon-Fri at 5:00PM. Weekends are for racing or climbing mountains, backpacking or ski mountaineering etc. November through March, he runs once a day 3 times per week because of the harsh weather conditions. From July to September, he races once every two weeks.

I have not set foot on a track in over seven years, but neither have I done much in regard to road racing. My motive for running is probably very unusual to most, and my training methods are unconventional by almost any standards. Ouray is in a narrow valley at 7,800 ft. with the mountains going to 14,149 ft. right from the streets of town. There is virtually no flat ground in or around town and Ouray has no track. Until three years ago, the nearest running companion or opponent was 300 miles away.

Since college, my training has been entirely mountain-oriented and races have been cross country and mountain races, with only a very few road races—even of these, at least half have been mountain road races. I would consider myself more of a mountain runner than anything else.

Philosophy: *Running began for me as a means of getting into the mountains around my home town of Ouray. After experiencing a great many aspects of the sport and* coming to know many runners both as teammates and adversaries, I find that this is still the prime motivation for my running.

The challenge of the hills with their steep, unrelenting grades, thick forests, barren alpine slopes, varied wildlike, changeable weather, and infinite variety of running surfaces is something which I cannot resist. As long as I live in mountains. I will continue to run upon them.

GARY TUTTLE

Gary was a top level runner at Humboldt State and, like a good wine, has improved with age. Most of his best times have come in the past several years including what he considers the best race of his life, a 7th-place finish in the World Cross Country Championships in Wales, England in 1976.

GARY ROBERT TUTTLE: Ventura, California. 5'9", 130. Born October 12, 1947 in Ventura. Occupation: Running shop-"Inside Track" and Fitness Classes. Works 48 hrs/wk. Married. Started running at age 15 and ran his first road race

at 17. Gary plans to race on the roads indefinitely, and his favorite distance there is 10 to 20k. His advisors are Jim Hunt from Humboldt State and Pete Petersons, Tobias Striders.

BEST MARKS: Mile, 4:08.9(69); Marathon, 2:15:15(77); 20 on track, 59:51(76); 1 hour, 12 miles, 811 yds(76); Steeple, 8:51(69).

TRAINING: Gary trains twice a day, every day, at 8:00a.m. and 3:30p.m. His longest ever run is the marathon. He likes to race on the roads once a month and on the track 2 or 3 times a month.

Mon—AM, easy 6 miles @ 6:30 pace. PM, easy 5 miles @ 6:30 pace.

Tues—AM, hilly 10 miles @ 5:30 pace. PM, easy 10 miles @ 6:30 pace.

Wed—AM, hilly 10 miles @ 5:30 pace. PM, fast flat 5 miles in 24-26 mins., or sometimes prior to Sunday race: 2-mile jog; 6x220 @ 31 w/110 jog, jog 220, 1x1000 on grass-jog 300, 6x220 @ 31 w/110 jog, jog 220, 1x1000 on grass, jog 400, 8x180 buildups with 5 seconds rest..

Thurs—AM, easy 6 miles @ 6:00 pace. PM, hilly 12 miles @ 5:30 pace—last mile 4:30.

Fri—AM, good effort 8 miles @ 5:15-5:30 pace. PM, hilly 7 miles @ 6:30.

Sat—AM, easy 6 miles at 6:30 pace. PM, easy 6 miles @ 6:30 pace.

Sun—AM, hilly 1:45-2:30 @ 8:00 pace. PM, easy 5 miles @ 7:30 pace.

Prior to the start of cross country and track Gary runs a little faster in his workouts. One change he has incorporated in his warmup routine is that he is starting to do some stretching for his hip. Does a moderated carbohydrate loading approximately 3x per year. His normal diet contains lots of fruits and vegetables with little meat. His only special training techniques are to run twice a week at a fast relaxed pace over 4-5 miles and lots of hills, while concentrating on a short, quick and relaxed stride.

I run because of fitness, competition, travel, social activity, self-satisfaction, and because I'm naturalist at heart. I feel good when I'm moving—makes feel like I'm doing something constructive and completes me as a person.

CRAIG VIRGIN

Steadily, Craig has come to dominate the distance races from 10,000 meters to 10-miles in the U.S. Long a factor on the track, 1979 was the year Virgin first turned serious attention to road racing. Runner-up to H. Lindsay in the Road Runner of the Year balloting, Virgin proved that one can race effectively both on the track and the road. And with his measured approach to the sport, he should be a factor for many years to come.

CRAIG VIRGIN: Lebanon, Illinois. 5-10, 137. Born August 2, 1955. Occupation: Promotions/Public Relations Consultant, working 30-50 hours per week. Single. Started competing at age 14 and road racing at 16. He plans to continue competitive road racing until age 30-32. Virgin is advised by Gary Wieneke and Pete Petersons. His favorite distance is "breakfast."

BEST MARKS: 3000, 7:48.2(79), 2-miles, 8:25.3(76); 5000, 13:23.3(79); 10k, 27:39.4AR(79); road marks: 10k, 28:31; 10-miles(short), 46:33; Marathon, 2:14:40.

TRAINING: Virgin trains twice a day, every day, with his morning run usually consisting of 4 miles. *It's not as much as a lot of guys do, but I work into it. Also, I'm a little stiff in the mornings.* His longest-ever training run has been a marathon, and his preferred racing frequency is 2-3 times per month.

Craig plans his training along a three-cycle pyramid, lasting 11 months of the year. After a very easy September, which includes two weeks entirely off from running, Virgin begins with a base building period from Oct. 1-March 1. From the middle of March to early June, Virgin adds a greater speed component to his base work. From the end of June to the end of August is given over to racing. Following are some of the workouts Virgin feels are the bread-and-butter of the various cycles. He notes that "the recovery day is fully as important as the hard workout days."

OCTOBER 1-MARCH 1

The workout week may include any or all of:
1) Long run of 15-20 miles.
2) Fartlek run of 10-12 miles.
3) Hill workout, doing repeats up to 300-400 meter hill.
4) Race, either high caliber or local.
5) Recovery day with 4 miles in the morning and 8-10 miles in the evening, as he feels.

1) Substitute a track workout for one hill workout or fartlek workout. Do 400s, 600s, 800s at 62-66 second pace.

2) Begin to do quicker stuff in the middle of April, retaining an occasional hill workout through the end of May. After May, do few hill workouts, but retain the fartlek. By mid-May, Virgin is doing 2 track workouts per week.

3) Craig says that three of his favorite track workouts during this period are: 12 x 440 in 63-65 with a 220 jog, moving the last 3 in 56-59; and, 12 x 220 with a 220 jog recovery; and, 1 x mile in 4:06-4:09, 880 in 1:56 (in 1980, Craig hopes to be able to add a 1320 to this workout).

About his training, the American 10k record holder comments: *I think my major weakness lies in the "polishing" stage of my program. I am seeking advice on how I can peak more effectively for the big race, and perhaps have a better finishing kick. As for any "unique" training techniques, I think the only major thing is that I have always stressed quality over quantity.*

Another area Virgin wants to work on is his flexibility. *I'm lazy about it. My schedule is too demanding to have the time to do it, but I'm going to work on it. If I learn to polish my speed and flexibility, then my finishing speed will improve.*

Craig works out with weights 2-3 times per week for 8-9 months of the year. He does pushups, situps, reverse situps, lat raises, exercises with a 40-lb. barbell, and 100 swings with 10-lb. dumbbells.

Running Philosophy: *Running is work to me most of the time. Perhaps once every two weeks I have a really fun workout; the rest of the time, it's hard work.*

Mainly, I run to race against myself, push myself to my limits, and secondly, to see how I stack up against other runners. I run for self-satisfaction, and I like the recognition that comes with it. I feel myself to be as much a performer as an athlete. I like to perform well, and be in the spotlight when racing. If I wanted to run for fitness, I could get by on 3-4 miles per week. But I'm interested in pushing beyond my limits.

FRITZ WATSON

Watson is an example of the late-starting road racer, who has talent, and who has been able to turn that talent into good times.

ROLAND (FRITZ) WATSON: Aptos, Calif. 5'11", 144. Born November 4, 1945 in Martinez, Calif. He is an Engineer working 40 hours a week. Divorced with 2 children. Fritz started competing and road racing at 29. He plans to continue as long as physically able.

BEST MARKS: Mile, 4:25(77); 2-mile, 9:37(77); 3-mile, 14:57(77); 10,000, 31:58(77); 10m road, 50:50(78); 20M 1:46:47(77); marathon, 2:21(77).

TRAINING: Fritz generally trains once a day, with two-a-days once or twice a week. He takes one day off before major races. His longest ever run has been the marathon. He prefers to race once or twice a month for shorter races and once a month for longer races with up to 3 marathons/yr.

Mon—PM, 11 miles @ medium pace (6:00-6:30).
Tues—PM, 8-11 miles @ medium pace.
Wed—11 miles hard (5:30). PM, 1 mile warmup, 10x440 with 440 jog in 72-75 whenever he feels up to it.
Thurs—PM, 8-11 miles easy (7:00).
Fri—11 miles medium pace.
Sat—10 miles all out on track (52-54 mins.); or nothing if racing the next day.
Sun—15-20 miles easy or race.
In building up for a marathon, Fritz will do two hard 10-mile runs twice a week for 3-4 weeks prior to the race. The week of the race he just does easy 5-6 mile runs.

Fritz supplements his running with yoga stretching before and after workouts and before bedtime. He eats a low-meat diet (fish, no beef except occasional liver), lots of fresh vegetables, whole wheat bread, brewers yeast, cod liver oil, 1½ gms. vit. C daily. He has high carbohydrates 3 days prior to marathons. He eats two pancakes and syrup the morning of the race and drinks ERG before race and during the early stages. . . *I generally follow a hard-easy approach, trying to allow adequate recovery between hard runs.*

RON WAYNE

Ron ran 5 sub-2:20 marathons in 1977, more than anyone else except Bill Rodgers. A running businessman, Wayne puts something back into the sport through his support of the running community.

RON WAYNE: Alameda, Calif. 5'8", 134. Born August 16, 1949 in Boston, Mass. He is in sporting goods retail sales working 30-50 hours a week. Married. Ron started competing and road racing at 16. At this point he sees no end in sight to competing. His favorite distance is the marathon. He is self-coached but feels he needs one.

BEST MARKS: Mile, 4:09.4i(70); 2-mile, 9:01.7i(70); 3-mile, 13:58(73); 15k Road, 46:05(77); 6-mile, 28:57(74); 25k Road, 1:18:52(74); Marathon, 2:15:04(77).

TRAINING: Ron trains twice at 6:30AM and 4:00PM Monday through Saturday and once Sunday at 7:30AM. His longest ever run is 27 miles and he prefers to run 15-20 races per year.
Mon—AM, 13 miles (LSD). PM, 8 miles (LSD).
Tues—AM, Same. PM, 2 miles (LSD), 12x440(75), 2 miles (LSD).
Wed—AM, Same. PM, 8 miles (LSD).
Thurs—AM, Same, PM, 2 miles (LSD), 6x880(2:30), 2 miles (LSD).
Fri—AM, Same, PM, 8 miles (LSD).
Sat—AM, Same, PM, 8 miles (LSD).
Sun—AM, 25 miles at 6:30 pace.

Training is geared strictly for marathons. Goal is to build to 140-150 miles per week which develops confidence. Race the 2 weekends before marathon preferably at 10-15 mile distance.

Ron supplements his running with daily leg stretching and 20 pushups after each workout. In warm weather he jumps in the swimming pool and kicks after long runs. Ron supplements his diet with a large amount of bread and cereals in addition to 6 protein pills daily (Body Ammo I). Before marathons he does a 5-day carbohydrate loading of 2½ days of protein and fats and 2½ days of increasing the carbohydrates.

As I grew up I was always involved in competition athletics—Baseball, Football, Basketball. While preparing for H.S. Basketball, I decided to run cross country my Junior year and found I enjoyed distance running. I had success in running my Senior year by winning the Mass. and New England Cross Country Championships finishing undefeated for the season. I enjoyed competition and success which is still true today. Furthermore, my running success helps business in my sporting goods store, provides opportunities for travel, and as a fringe benefit, a healthy body.

JEFF WELLS

After a very competent college track career at Rice University, Jeff burst onto the road racing scene in the 1978 Boston Marathon by almost catching Bill Rodgers in the last few yards of the closest race in Boston history.

JEFFERY HAROLD WELLS: Dallas, Texas. 5'11½", 140. Born May 25, 1954 at Madisonville, Texas. Student. Single. Jeff started competing at age 12. His first road race was at 18 and didn't run his second until age 21. He plans to run and race all his life but not always seriously. His favorite distance is the marathon. Coached by Harry Johnson.

BEST MARKS: 1500m, 3:47.6(78); mile, 4:05.7(76); 2-mile, 8:40.0(74); 3-mile, 13:25.1(76); 5000m, 13:44(78); 10,000m, 28:47.4(76); 10k-road, 28:39(77); 20k-road, 61:40(78); marathon, 2:10:15(78).

TRAINING: Jeff runs twice-a-day usually, except during school semesters when there are time limitations and then he cuts to 304 double sessions per week. His longest ever run is the marathon. He prefers to race 2-3 times per month.

Mon—AM, 10k as he feels. PM, 5k warmup, intervals, such as 1400, 1600, 1200, 800 plus light fartlek.
Tues—AM, 3k(early class). PM, 20k as he feels.
Wed—AM, 0. PM, 40k(pace varies, maybe 6-7:00 per mile.)
Thurs—AM, 3k. PM, 10k easy.
Fri—AM, 0. PM, light intervals, like 10x300(45) + 10x200(30), plus a 5k warmup and cooldown.
Sat—AM, 20k @ 5:10 mile pace. PM, 5k easy.
Sun—20k as he feels. (This is an ideal week.)

Jeff adjusts his training the last two months before a marathon. He does more speed work as the summer track season approaches, and takes a couple of weeks a year very easy plus a very easy week after marathons.

I train under Harry Johnson, who has a fartlek workout called Holmer fartlek; it's divided into 4 parts with a jog in between the parts. Distances vary between 50 meters and 800 meters. Also, I do some intervals up a slight hill. Also,

sometimes he has me do a run during an interval session, like 8 kilometers.

My basic motivation in running is to glorify Jesus Christ. All of our running ability is from God, and He deserves the credit for any success we have. I want to responsibly use the talent that God has given me to exalt Christ. There are other reasons subsumed under this one: I enjoy running, friendships through running, travel opportunities health benefits and relaxation.

TENA ANEX

Tena, well-known for her outstanding track credentials, has moved to the longer distances on the roads, with great success. Her best effort in the marathon came in placing 7th in the recent AAU women's marathon championships in a race in which 15 women broke the once magic barrier of 3 hours. This effort is just the beginning as she enjoys road racing and plans on competing 10 more years.

TENA ANEX: Sacramento, California. 5'8", 130. Born October 3, 1956 in Sacramento, California. Student at UC Davis. Started running at age 12 and road racing at 20. Her favorite distance is 20 miles.

BEST MARKS: 880, 2:12.0(72); mile, 4:50.9(72); 2-mile 10:22.6(73); 3-mile, 16:46(77); 20M, 2:03:56(76); marathon, 2:52:06(77).

TRAINING: Tena runs once a day year round, usually in the late afternoon (3:00-4:00). Two months before a big meet she will start double workouts for 5-6 weeks. Her longest ever run was 30 miles. Tena feels a marathon every 4 months and a 3-10 mile race every 2-4 weeks, are optimum.
Mon—AM, 5-6 miles @ 8:00 pace. PM, 6-7 miles fartlek running with mile pickups.
Tues—10 miles at 6:45 pace.
Wed—AM, 5-6 miles @ 8:00 pace. PM, 7 miles accelerating run from 7:00 to 6:00 pace at the end.
Thurs—8 mile run at 6:00 pace.
Fri—AM, 5-6 miles at 8:00 pace. PM, Interval work on grass: 880-1320-mile-1½ mile-1320-880 @ 5:20-6:00 pace.
Sat—7 to 8 miles @ 6:00-8:00 pace according to how she feels.
Sun—16 miles at 7:00 pace.

The month before and after a marathon are periods of less-intense training, particularly the month after. The second and third months following a marathon are the largest mileage months. Tena swims when her legs are sore or tight following running, and does situps daily, plus light weight training. She is a vegetarian, but otherwise follows no special diet. If a race is on Saturday, she switches the Wednesday and Friday workouts, and does the Sunday run at a pace which comes naturally.

I run because I like to, I'm a lifetime runner and set my goals accordingly. If I'm injured I don't run, so I'll be able to run later. I enjoy racing, to see all the people gathered to run. I particularly enjoy road racing because of the relaxed attitude enjoyment all seem to enjoy.

GAYLE BARRON

Winner of the 1978 Boston Marathon. Gayle races very well on what many would call a light training schedule. One of the reasons for her success is the wide-range of physical activities she participates in, which help make her generally fit and which promote a healthy, relaxed approach to training.

GAYLE STOCKS BARRON: Atlanta, Georgia. 5'5", 120. Born April 6, 1945 in Atlanta, Georgia. Occupation: Exercise Instructor working 20 hours/week. Married. She started road racing at age 27 and became competitively serious at 29. She plans to continue as long as it is enjoyable and without injuries. Her favorite distances are 15 miles and the marathon. She doesn't have a coach/advisor but wishes she did.

BEST MARKS: 440, 72; mile, 5:16; 2-mile 11:17; 10k, 35:40; 10M, 58:40; 15M, 1:34:20; 30k, 2:03:15; marathon, 2:47:40.

TRAINING: Gayle trains year round at 5:30 PM and runs every day except when her legs are fatigued. She occasionally runs twice a day. Her longest run is 30 miles. She prefers to race once a month, or twice at the most.
Mon—AM, 3 miles easy @ 9:00 pace. PM, 6 miles easy 7:00-7:30.
Tues—PM, Intervals or fartlek totaling 10 miles.
Wed—AM, 3 miles. PM, 8 miles 7:30 pace.
Thurs—14 miles @ 8:00 pace.
Fri—AM, 3 miles @ 9:00 pace. PM, 5 miles @ 8:00 pace.
Sat—Race, or do track workout totaling 10-12 miles.
Sun—20 miles @ 8:00 pace.
   Gayle begins a major mileage increase 5 weeks prior to a marathon and then tapers down afterwards to her normal load. She teaches yoga, and does stretching twice a day for flexibility. She also plays tennis, racquetball, swims and rides a bike often, as she feels it is important to deviate from running frequently. She eats a balanced diet, trying to avoid white flour and sugar and striving to consume more complex carbohydrates. She eats very little red meat, preferring fish,

chicken, eggs and dairy products. She bases her training on the hard/easy principle and tries to concentrate on quality rather than quantity mileage each week. She thinks it is important to listen to one's body and never push past fatigue.

I run because I enjoy it more than anything else I do. It gives me a chance to get off on my own and think about things that I have to do or things I've done. I also feel 100% better when I run at a moderate pace and don't overtrain. I am more of a Type A personality; (very active, impatient at times, easily excitable) and running has changed me quite a bit.

MARILYN BEVANS

While a relatively late starter, Marilyn has shown a wide range of distance running talent. May still be looking for her best event.

MARILYN THERESA BEVANS: Baltimore, Maryland. 5'5", 110. Born October 4, 1949 in Baltimore, Maryland. Occupation: Teacher working 32-40 hours/week. She started road racing at age 23 and plans to continue until her early 30s or longer. Her favorite distance is cross country in the 3 mile/5000meter range. She is self coached.

BEST MARKS: 440, 66(76); 1500m, 4:49(76); mile, 5:20(77); mile, 5:20(77); 3000m, 10:08(77); 3-mile, 17:45(77); 10,000m, 37:41(77); 5M, 30:10(76); 10M, 62:03(77); 20k, 1:23:26(76); half marathon, 1:24:31(76); 25k, 1:40:18(76); marathon, 2:51:29(77).

TRAINING: Marilyn trains 12 months a year, 7 days/week with an occasional day off. From September-June she runs at 5 PM or later and in July-August at 9 AM. Her longest ever run is 26 miles 385 yards. She likes to race twice a month, except during the fall when she prefers a race per week.
Mon—Mile pace work.
Tues—5-10 miles easy.
Wed—Intervals such as 220s, 440s or 880s.
Thurs—5-10 easy.
Fri—5-8 miles hard and fast.
Sat—18-22 miles slow.
Sun—5-10 miles easy. This is the routine for the month leading to a marathon. For shorter races, she does one day-a-week of short (100-440) repeats, one day of long intervals (880), and one run as long and as hard as possible.
Marilyn intensifies her training during the fall, late summer and early spring. She does stretching, situps, push ups and Tai-Kwan-Do (Korean martial art) to supplement her running. She does carbohydrate loading before marathons, doesn't drink sodas or eat meat, at anytime, but does eat a lot of fruit.

I run because of the peace and quiet that is part of running the many miles of training. I get to think over problems and possibly solve them. I also enjoy the feeling of strength that follows a good work out or race.

Dorothy is a track and field coach who practices what she preaches. In spite of a relatively late start towards serious competition, she has achieved an excellent marathon of 2:50:44 in the Mayor Daley Marathon in Chicago.

DORIS BROWN-HERITAGE

Member of the U.S. Olympic team in '68, Doris has been a real pioneer in women's running. If you think women are discriminated against now, you should have seen what it was like during Heritage's prime. While she now subordinates her running to her coaching career, Doris nonetheless is still able to race at a fairly high level, and more importantly, she still enjoys it as much as ever.

DORIS ELAINE (BROWN) HERITAGE: Seattle, Washington. 5'4", 112. Born September 17, 1942 in Tacoma, Washington. Occupation: College Assistant Professor and coach. Married. Started competing at age 16. She plans to always run competitive road races. Her coach is Ken Foreman.

BEST MARKS: 440, 55.0; 880, 2:02.2; 1500m, 4:13.8; mile, 4:39; 6-mile, 33:00; marathon, 2:47.

TRAINING: Doris has a high degree of job-responsibility and is also a member of the USOC which prevents her from systematic training. She runs five miles almost every morning. Sporadically, she can fit in an afternoon workout which might be 8-10 miles of hill fartlek or 8-10 miles in a track session. She considers herself "retired" from big time competition and is more of a recreational road runner.

Supplementary exercise: *Doris does cross country skiing when she teaches it in alternate years. She stretches about 20 minutes per day and does some weight training with her conditioning classes.*

Diet: *She avoids sugar, salt, refined flour and preservatives, and eats a lot of fruit, vegetables and meat. Not a part of her diet are ham, butter or much milk, other than yogurt and buttermilk.*

Right now I'm frustrated because my feeling of obligation that an athlete should take advantage of input opportunities with governing bodies (USOC) has found me home 1 of the past 9 weekends. So my job is affected (as a coach) and I can only cut my own running (or a divorce) would result). But at the end of the quadrennial, I'll run for enjoyment again! I like to run, especially if I have somewhere to go—visit a friend, get to school, etc. I'd rather run than anything else in my spare time. I also like to train toward something; i.e., international cross country, two-mile relay for outdoor nationals or a marathon. I find I enjoy running more when I put myself on the line occasionally. I don't know yet how to adjust for those 200,000 road runners as opposed to "a few of us" several years ago.

MARTY COOKSEY

One of the most talented female athletes in any sport, Marty has yet to reach her maximum. Winner of the Avon Marathon in 1978, and second at Boston in 1979. Her high intensity training will either make her or break her. Cooksey is an eloquent argument for longer distances than 1500 meters at the Olympic Games.

MARTHA KIMBERLY COOKSEY: Orange, California. 5'5", 106. Born July 18, 1954 in Spencer, Iowa. She is a part time employee in a running shoe store working 20-30 hours a week. Single. She started road racing at 22. She plans to continue indefinitely. Her favorite distances are 15-30 kilometers and the marathon. Her coach is Brian M. Oldham.

BEST TIMES: 10k, 34:00(78); 15k, 51:36(78); 30k, 1:56:16(78); Marathon, 2:43:33(79); 5M, 27:43(78); 8M, 43:24(78).

TRAINING: Marty usually trains twice a day year round unless prohibited by traveling or is resting before races. Her longest ever run was 32 miles. She prefers to race 10-15 times per year in groups with some relaxed training time in between.
Mon—AM, 10 miles @ 6:00 pace. PM, and noon 4 miles @ 8:00 pace.
Tues—AM, 12 miles exploring. PM, 3-5 miles gentle relaxed pace.
Wed—AM, 10 miles @ 7:00 pace. PM, 5-6 miles on track with Lydiard type technique drills followed by hard steady laps and then intervals of 220s and recovery 440s and a cooldown.
Thurs—AM, 10 miles @ 7:30 pace (hills). Noon, 4-5 miles fartlek. PM, 4-5 miles slow social running.
Fri—AM, 11-12 miles @ 6:45 pace. PM, 6-7 miles slow (8:00).
Sat—Same as Wednesday.
Sun—AM, At least 2 hours of continuous running about 16 miles. PM, 2-4 miles of relaxed social type running.

Most of the training is done in hills around home, along the coast highway, interesting parks or neighborhoods. Variety is emphasized, company desired when quality allows. Flexibility to body signs is a must. This schedule is adaptable for variable race preparation.

Training Cycles: *I recognize the fact that body and mind cannot achieve and maintain at peak levels all year around. We (my coach Brian and I) allow for less intense training periods when needed to prevent overstress and design specific training for the kind of race I have chosen (i.e., altitude, distance, terrain, etc.).*

Supplementary exercises: *I include some yoga-type stretching, situps and pushups as regular supplementation to running. I especially enjoy swimming and body surfing when opportunity allows. Also cycling on a regular basis. Some occasional sand volleyball and water sports.*

Diet: *I adhere to a natural foods vegetarian diet which includes a few egg and dairy products occasionally. Have experimented with fasting before races but follow no particular regimen before a race. I do eat very lightly before a race and nothing the morning of race.*

Training Techniques: *We take care to listen to the whole person while training; being sensitive to mental and emotional states as well as the physical well-being. Though some basic training schedule is required, we take great care in creating variety and flexibility in our training. On most training runs I try to develop a "feeling" for how I want to run, as opposed to a structured or scientific aspect and can be analyzed and broken down. Being aware of those factors and trying to incorporate good running form is important. But while running I usually "feel" as opposed to "think" about form.*

Philosophy: *I run to create a daily mental and physical challenge, which having been achieved sets me free to operate at a higher more finely-attuned level. This is both emotional and physical. I use races as an incentive to train creatively and specifically for; and as a further, more intense confrontation to my physical and mental limits.*

PENNY DEMOSS

Second at Boston in 1978, DeMoss is coming back from heel surgery. Her success has come from consistent 100-mile weeks over a period of years. Penny is an athlete who has contributed much to the sport through her art, AAU activities, and race promotion.

PENNY DE MOSS: Los Altos, California. 5'5", 120. Born January 4, 1950 in San Francisco, California. Penny is an artist working 35 hours per week. Married. Started competing and road racing at age 23. She plans to continue indefinitely. Her favorite distance is 10 miles. Self-coached.

BEST MARKS: 1 mile(track), 5:36; Roads: 5k, 17:50 enroute to 10k, 36:37(78); 15k, 57:58 enroute to 25k, 1:38:02(77); 30k, 2:04:23(76); 20 miles, 2:06:10 enroute to marathon, 2:45:34(78); 50k, 3:48:27(76).

TRAINING: Penny trains the same all year; twice a day on weekdays and once a day on weekends. Her longest ever run was 33 miles and she prefers to race every two weeks. Monday through Friday her AM runs are 5 miles at 8:00 pace.
Mon—PM, 10 miles according to feel.
Tues—PM, 10 miles @ 7:00-7:15 pace.
Wed—PM, 12 miles total with 3 repeat miles (5:40-6:00).
Thurs—PM, 10 miles easy.
Fri—PM, same as Wednesday if not racing on Sunday.
Sat—AM, 10-15 miles easy.
Sun—Race or 16-20 miles @ 7:15 pace.

Penny does Sheehan's basic 6 stretching exercises and 50 situps each day, with 25 using a 5 lb. weight. She always uses carbo-loading for marathons but not always with the depletion phase. Penny runs because, *It feels good—keeps me healthy, etc.*

DOROTHY DOOLITTLE

Dorothy is that rarity in the coaching profession: a coach who has integrated her own training into her coaching to the benefit of both.

DOROTHY DOOLITTLE: Columbia, Missouri. 5'0", 90. Born October 17, 1946 in Taylor, Texas. Occupation: Women's track and field, cross country coach, working 50-60 hours per week. Married. Started competing seriously on the roads at age 27. She plans to run for life. Her favorite distance is the marathon and she is self-coached.

BEST MARK: Marathon 2:50:44.

TRAINING: Dorothy trains 12 months a year, 6 days/week. She does a long run on Sunday, and trains twice on Monday through Thursday. Friday is a one-session easy day and Saturday is for rest. Her summer mileage is about 50-55 miles per week and the rest of the year 60-65. Her longest run is the marathon. She prefers to race the marathon 3 times per year and race shorter distances frequently to stay sharp.

Mon—AM, 5 miles steady @ 7:00-6:30 pace. PM, same as AM.
Tues—AM, 6x1320(4:30) or 8x880(2:50). PM, 5 miles steady @ 7:00-7:15.
Wed—AM, 8 miles steady @ 6:30-6:45. PM, 3 miles steady @ 6:15-6:30.
Thurs—AM, 8 miles 6:45-7:15. PM, 4 miles fartlek.
Fri—AM, 6 miles @ 7:00. PM, rest.
Sat—Rest day.
Sun—AM, 14-20 miles @ 7:00. PM, rest.

One month prior to a marathon, Dorothy increases her mileage to 65-70/week and then tapers way down the week of the race after a depletion run a full week before. She has weight trained in the past and plans to resume. Attempts are made to cut down on refined sugar, flour and on beef and pork.

I enjoy running. It has also been very informative in my coaching career. Once one has experienced some workouts, injuries, etc., it makes one more aware of the problems, benefits, etc.

MIKI GORMAN

Winner of Boston, New York, and other prestigious marathons, Miki is not only the best all-around Masters road racer in the country, she is also among the best of any age.

MIKI GORMAN: Los Angeles, California. 5'11", 90. Born August 9, 1935 in China. Her occupation is housewife. Miki started competing at age 33 and road racing at 37. She plans to continue as long as she can. Her favorite distances are 10k and longer. Her coach/advisors are Laszlo Tabori and Dr. Myron Shapiro.

BEST MARKS: 1500m, 4:39(77); 3000m, 10:04(77); 5000m, 16:59(77); 10,000m, 35:45(77); 10k-xc, 35:28; 20k(road), 1:15(77); 25k(road), 1:38:40(77); 30k(road), 1:57:30(76); marathon, 2:39:11(76).

TRAINING: Miki trains once a day most of the year but adds some double sessions 2-4 days a week in the month prior to a major marathon. Her longest ever run is 100 miles.
Mon—AM, 10-15 miles according to feel.
Tues—AM, 5 miles jog @ 8:00 pace. PM, 10-12 miles, intervals.
Wed—AM, 10-15 miles according to feel.
Thurs—AM, 3-5 mile jog. PM, 10+ miles, 6:00-7:00 pace.
Fri—AM, 10-15 miles according to feel.
Sat—AM, 20 miles @ 8:00 pace.
Sun—AM, 10-15 as she feels. Her training isn't always the same.

Miki uses carbohydrate loading. She runs because it feels good and she likes competition.

JACQUELINE HANSEN

Jacqueline Hansen was the first American woman with strong track ability to run the marathon seriously. Her talent and hard work led to one of the major breakthroughs in women's marathoning, a stunning world record of 2:38:19 in 1975. Her achievement clearly demonstrated that women can run the marathon at high speed, and not merely "cover the distance."

JACQUELINE ANN HANSEN: Topanga, California. 5'3", 112. Born November 20, 1948 in Binghamton, New York. Occupation: Distributor of ERG with variable hours. Married. Started running at 22 and road racing at 24. Her coach is Laszlo Tabori.

BEST MARKS: 440r, 61(72); 880, 2:16(72); 1500, 4:28(76); 2-mile, 10:28(75); 5,000, 16:55(75); 6-mile, 34:24(74), 15k (road), 52:15(74); 1 hour, 10 miles 243 yds(75); 25k (road), 1:35:39(76); 30k (road), 1:54:57(76); marathon, 2:38:19(75).

TRAINING: Jacqueline's longest run is 28 miles done on her 28th birthday. In her "competitive season," road races in fall and track races in spring, she likes to race 3 times per month for a period of 1½ to 2 months. Her training is best described in her own words:

I particularly have trouble when describing training techniques, frequency of training runs and races. This is because it all varies so much, has not been the same every season and is still changing as I continue to learn more methods. In the past 7 years I've been training competitively, I have always been fond of doing short, easy ± mile runs in the morning as a supplement to my regular workouts. This of course varies more or less in mileage and is not a daily routine. My logs show I do this maybe 50% of the time. Until recently, my workouts could be outlined as: intervals 3 times a week, moderate runs of 8-12 miles 3 times a week and one long run a week or a race instead. Presently, however, I have been experimenting with Lydiard's schedules and may continue to do so for awhile.

During the fall and Winter months, Hansen runs more mileage (up to 100 mile/wk) in preparation for marathons and other road races during that time of year. During track season she does more intensity on the track and less miles.

She supplements her running with yoga-style stretching. Her diet tends to be conscious of good nutrition, avoiding fat, sugar and artificial ingredients. She eats a lot of fresh fruit and vegetables and consumes poultry and fish rather than other meat. Jacqueline does the complete depletion/loading of carbohydrates prior to marathons.

I suppose I run to satisfy an inner desire to run, to maintain good shape, and to fulfill a potential I recognize within me.

JUDY GUMBS-LEYDIG

Judy started running for fitness with a group at work in 1974. After giving a few races a try, her talent became obvious. She has raced very well in the Northern California-San Francisco Bay Area, and recently placed 4th in the Women's National AAU marathon championships in 2:50:40 for one of her competitive highlights.

JUDY ANN GUMBS-LEYDIG: San Mateo, California. 5'8", 130. Born April 1, 1951 in San Francisco. Occupation: Physical Therapist working 40 hours per week. Married. Started competing at age 23 in road races. She plans to run as long as physically able. Her favorite distance is in the 15k-10 mile range. Her advisor is her husband, Jack Leydig.

BEST MARKS: Mile, 5:29(77); 5M, 29:15(77); 10k, 37:35(77); 15k, 57:20*(77); 10M, 1:02:50(75); 20k, 1:17:05*(77); 25k, 1:36:35(77); 30k, 2:03:50(76); marathon, 2:50:40. *set enroute to 25k.

TRAINING: Judy trains daily, and twice daily about 4 days per week. Her longest ever run is the marathon. Preferred racing frequency is: once a week for 3-10 mile races, every other week for 20 to 30k races, and twice a year for marathons. Thus far she has pointed for a couple of marathon races each year, making special preparations for these.

She starts with 3 weeks of 80 miles per week with one long (20+) run and one interval session. The other mileage is mostly 7 miles at noon and 5-10 miles in the evening. This progresses to 100 miles/wk for 2 weeks and the interval work is volume work, like 20x220 or 20x440 or 10x880. She cuts back to 80 miles/wk for 3 weeks, as before, then tapers with two weeks of 50-60 miles and two weeks of 30-40 miles. Judy runs short (10k or less) races during this time. She does interval work twice a week such as 440s, 880s or miles @ 85=90% effort with a short rest. Sometimes she does hill repeats instead of the intervals. The last week is much easier and one workout includes some 110s. The rest of the year she runs 40-50 miles/wk and races about 3 times a month.

She does a hill workout once a month at this time. In the coming year, Judy is going to point more for the cross country and track seasons and will change her training accordingly.

Judy stretches after each training session and does weight training three times per week. During her off season, she stops interval training and does fartlek sessions instead, emphasizing pushing the uphills.

I run to stay in shape which gives me the physical and psychological well-being I need to be happy with myself. The competition is the kick or the ego boost one needs. This is especially true for a woman who is in the limelight usually by her mere presence, since the male population outnumbers the female by about 10 to 1.

PEG NEPPEL

Neppel is one of the first women runners who has gone from an excellent collegiate track program, to a brief but successful venture at road racing, before moving on to other interests outside of the running sphere. Former world record holder at 10,000 meters.

PEGGY SUZANNE NEPPEL: Ames, Iowa. 5'6", 121. Born August 16, 1953 in San Antonio, Texas. Occupation: student working 20 hours per week. Peggy started competing at 16 and road racing at 22. Her favorite distance is 10,000m and her coach is Chris Murray. She would like to be self-coached but doesn't think it is as successful an approach.

BEST MARKS: 880, 2:14(75); mile, 4:44(75); 1500m, 4:21(76), 3,000m, 9:17(75); 5,000m, 15:52; 10,000m(33:14) track and 34:15 road both in 77.

TRAINING: During the fall and spring she runs 10 times a week at 7 AM and 4 PM. She runs 6 times a week in winter at 4 PM and 7 times a week in the summer when it is coolest. Her longest ever run is 16 miles. Peg prefers to race once a month unless she is in good shape and then more often.

During the fall and spring Peggy's training is supplemented with morning runs of 4 easy miles. Afternoon workouts begin with base type training and give way to an interval program. She has one rest day (6-8 miles fun and easy) and one mileage day per week to supplement the interval program. Neppel does long intervals with 12-16 repeats and builds to quality repeats with a longer rest during the racing season.

Peggy bicycles for transportation. She thinks weight training and stretching are the most beneficial supplementary exercises. Before racing she eats enjoyable, easily digestible foods. While in training she tries to avoid overeating.

I find it very difficult to train when I pay attention or meditate on my training activities. Therefore, I try to be mentally involved with other activities rather than being preoccupied with training (racing requires a bit more meditation at the appropriate time).

LEAL-ANN REINHART

The 1977 AAU marathon champion, Leal enjoyed great success under the training methods of Laszlo Tabori. Now living in Berkeley, Calif., Reinhart plans to concentrate on the shorter distances before going back to the marathon.

LEAL-ANN REINHART: Northridge, California. 5'4½", 110. Born October 11, 1947 in Oakland, California. Occupation: Sports promotion working 30-40 hours/week. Married. She started road racing at age 27. She plans to continue as long as she enjoys it. Her favorite distance is the marathon and she is self-coached.

BEST TIME: 5000m(ex), 16:59(76); 10M(road), 62:06(77); 10,000m (road), 37:06(76); 15k(road), 57:39(76); marathon, 2:46:34(77).

TRAINING: Leal-Ann generally trains once a day in the afternoon (3-6) except when training for a marathon; then she trains twice a day. She takes off about 30 days a year to rest or heal up minor injuries. Her longest run was 27 miles and she prefers to race once a month.

Mon—PM, 7-12 miles as she feels, usually 7:00-8:00 pace.

Tues—PM, 10-15 miles of varying pace intervals.

Wed—1-1½ hours easy running; or ½ hour easy, ½ fresh; or hard fartlek and ½ hour varied pace, comfortable.

Thurs—10-15 miles of intervals like Tuesday, but shorter runs with more sets if racing on Saturday.

Fri—7-12 miles according to feel; or 3-5 miles easy with shake ups if racing.

Sat—1-1½ hour run; or 10-15 miles of intervals or 3-5 warmup if racing Sunday.

Sun—Race of 15-21 miles, run at varying pace (6:30-8:00)

Before a marathon I train twice a day for 6-8 weeks—6 miles AM—8-16 miles PM—about a 16-mile-per-day average. The intervals are longer, e.g., sets of 3 laps rather than sets of 220s, etc.

She tries to remember to stretch but finds *it's a drag,* and tends to forget it more often than remember.

I rarely eat beef—mostly chicken, fish, soup and salad. I carbo-load (including depletion) before a marathon. In general I try to limit sugar and fat intake. Before a race I always try to err on the side of rest—I think a lot of road runners have "mile-itis" and are always overtrained, never really fresh.

I run because I love all the attendant benefits. It is a micro-therapy for me—I get all my best thinking & problem-solving/creating done on the run. I am not very fond of racing. If I never raced again I would continue to run. I can really get into two or three races per year. Those are usually really peak experiences for me. I push myself to my own limits in those situations and am totally oblivious to others around me. I do not consider myself competitive—I get no adrenalin charge to "beat" someone—just me against myself.

JULIE SHEA

Julie is an example of the successful age-group runner who has blossomed on the roads, while still achieving consistently high-quality times on the track. Shea has become one of America's best road racers and cross-country runners. She can always be counted on to finish among the leaders.

JULIE ANNA SHEA: Raleigh, North Carolina. 5'10½", 129. Born May 3, 1959 in Raleigh, North Carolina. Student. She started competing and road racing at age 8. She plans to continue several more years. Her favorite distance is 10,000m. Her coach is Mike Shea, father.

BEST MARKS: 800m, 2:12; mile, 4:43; 3-miles, 15:49; 10,000m, 35:04; 10M, 56:08.

TRAINING: Julie usually runs twice a day year-round except when tapering for a big race. Her longest ever run was the Charlestown 15-mile Distance classic. Racing frequency preference is once a month. She runs 4 miles in the morning Monday through Saturday around 5:30 pace. Monday through Friday afternoons Julie does her coach's workouts, and on Sunday she runs 10-12 miles under 6:00 pace. In the spring, speed running is done 2-3 times a week, e.g., 440s. She usually lifts weight for 10 minutes 4-5 days per week. She also swims a ½ mile 4-5 days a week. Julie likes to train, and enjoys the feeling of running stride-for-stride with another runner. The pain that comes with racing isn't as much fun, but she finds that once the race is over, the hurting doesn't seem so bad. One of Shea's favorite things about running is the trips when she is *lucky enough to get them.* There will be many more in the future.